Apology

For Kathy —
Shine on!

Sheila

Apology

The Importance and Power
of Saying "I'm sorry"

sheila quinn simpson

BALCONY PUBLICATIONS

Balcony Publications
P.O. Box 2032
Gaylord, Michigan 49734

Printed in the United States of America
Project coordinated by To The Point Solutions
Cover and interior design by Mary Jo Zazueta

PUBLISHER'S CATALOGING-IN-PUBLICATION DATA
Simpson, Sheila Quinn.

Apology : the importance and power of saying "i'm sorry" / Sheila Quinn Simpson. — Gaylord, Mich. : Balcony Publications, 2005.
     p. ; cm.

  ISBN 0-9755497-0-7
  Library of Congress Control Number: 2004109613

    1. Apologizing. 2. Remorse. 3. Guilt. 4. Forgiveness. Emotions. I. Title. II. Importance and power of saying "I'm sorry".

BF575.A75 S56 2005   2004109613
152.4--dc22   0410

10 9 8 7 6 5 4 3 2 1

To all those who do not yet understand
the importance of their apology . . .
to all those who do not yet know how to apologize . . .
and to all those who yearn to hear
words of sincere apology . . .
This book is written for your awareness, your courage,
and your healing.

Contents

Acknowledgments

This book could not have been written without the inspiration, confidence, encouragement, and lessons that have been the graces and Spirit in my life.

I gratefully acknowledge my husband, Charlie;

Our children, David, Colin and Brianna, for enriching my life in immeasurable ways, and for the precious gift of knowing that you are always in my balcony;

My wonderful family circle, from whom I have received the gifts of unconditional love, generosity, honesty, laughter, and confidence;

My friends, far and near, whose names would expand this book by one hundred pages, who have inspired me and challenged me in ways that resulted in my deeper reflection about life and risk and love;

Mary Backlund, friend, artist, and author, who gave the seeds of this book the opportunity to grow and blossom;

Mary Jo Zazueta, my editor, for sifting my words and shaking out the best of my intent; and

You, for discovering this book and trusting, without knowing yet where it will lead you.

The triangular Celtic knots throughout this book are used as symbols of the dynamic, complex Life forces. Each knot represents our spiritual, physical, and emotional connection . . . without beginning or end . . . just as all of our lives are uniquely interwoven with others.

Our actions . . . our decisions . . . our choices . . . affect others . . . for generations.

I am grateful to friend and mentor Jan Cotant for the inspiration to use this special symbol for *Apology*, and for her artwork of the Celtic knots; and to my friend Jean Parker, for providing the graphic files necessary.

Introduction

It is not by random coincidence that you have found this book . . . and that this book has found you. Whatever your personal situation and life experience, this book is intended to awaken your internal wisdom, and remind you of a truth that you inwardly already know: There is healing power in the words "I'm sorry" which benefit both the giver of an apology and the receiver of the gift of these words.

The subject of apology seems to be invisible in society; yet the need for apology is everywhere.

You may harbor a lingering regret about something you once said or did . . . or something good that you did not say or do. You still can do something about that.

Perhaps you have a secret pain from a deep need to hear words of apology from someone. You still can heal through that pain.

I cannot explain what motivated me to write this book other than an inner calling to do so.

Throughout much of my life, I have been drawn to stories in which people's lives would have been forever changed for the better if they had only received or extended a sincere apology. It sounds so simple—but in reality, apologizing is often a difficult action to take.

As I write, I am acutely aware that many strings are attached to the topic of apology. Any one of these strings can resonate in your heart, mind, and spirit. Feelings that you thought were quiet may become restless, tender, or raw.

Take heart. Keep reading.

Know that I have your well-being in mind. Each page is intended to confirm the power that you possess to wisely decide to change your own life, and the lives of others, with a sincere apology.

The focus of this book is not to make you feel guilty . . . or more wounded. My intention is to increase your awareness. And with awareness, there is hope . . . for change . . . for growth . . . for renewal.

This message is my gift to you.

Chapter One

> There is only one thing harder in this
> world than forgiving . . . and it is to ask
> for forgiveness armed only with
> 'I'm sorry.'
>
> ~ ERMA BOMBECK

M ANY BOOKS, articles, and other media focus
on the healing aspects of *forgiveness* . . .
emotionally, physically, and spiritually.
Rarely discussed or explored, however, are the healing
properties of a sincere *apology*, which you have the
power to extend. Power in this context means the
strength within you, where spirit, truth, and
wholeness reside.

People often equate the words *forgiveness* and
apology, and use them interchangeably. They are
distinctly different actions.

Forgiveness often flows *after* an apology has been
extended. Sometimes, forgiveness is an act of inner

self-strength, a deliberate action one takes to heal and thrive without ever receiving an apology.

Forgiveness stems from the person who has been hurt. Apology stems from the person whose conduct caused the hurt.

By definition, apology is a written or spoken admission of error, discourtesy, or regret. Apology is not a feeling. It is an action—a meaningful extension of yourself to another. Apology takes responsibility. By withholding or offering the gift of an apology, you can forever change lives.

The fire of my belief in the importance of apology was fanned in part many years ago while watching the movie *Love Story*. In the film, one of the main characters declared to the other, "Love means never having to say you're sorry." This line was one of the movie's leading promotional phrases, and many people thought the words were profound. As a college student at the time, I thought the words were foolish.

"I'm sorry" is one of *the* most important expressions of love . . . love for one's wholeness and integrity, and love for the well-being of others. For years I have been drawn to stories about lives that could have been improved, had sorrows eased, and relationships saved, if only someone had been courageous enough to extend a heartfelt apology.

Any violation in which human value and dignity are compromised or diminished requires an apology.

People have been harmed in many ways: a loved one is injured or killed in a drunk-driving accident; someone is mired in an abusive relationship; hurtful words are spoken that cannot be retrieved; a partner chooses to be unfaithful and subsequent lies occur. The list of situations is long.

In many cases, when an apology is not forthcoming, new cycles of isolation, anger, distrust, and harm result.

Your actions and words significantly impact the lives of others . . . families, neighbors, coworkers, and strangers who cross your path . . . or the path of those whom you have offended. People struggle, often by sheer will power, trying to forgive or forget so that they can begin to heal. How helpful it would be for their recovery, and your integrity, if they heard— sincerely—the words "I'm sorry."

It is a common misconception that to apologize reflects weakness. On the contrary, apologizing takes strength, courage, trust, character, hope, and humility. These values can restore communication, enhance relationships, lead to personal growth, and bring freedom from the burden of holding back power that needs to be released.

Apology is an important *action* of mind, will, and heart that benefits both the person who receives the gift of apology and the person who apologizes. Few other expressions allow us to move through the quicksand of sorrow, anger, hurt, and bitterness . . . to the healing pasture where greater understanding, forgiveness, relief, and reconciliation can nourish our bodies, minds, and souls.

Chapter Two

> Men occasionally stumble over the truth,
> but most of them pick themselves up and
> hurry off as if nothing happened.
>
> ~ WINSTON CHURCHILL

THE AWARENESS of the need to apologize is uniquely different than *regret* or *remorse*. Regret and remorse are feelings within you about your choices and actions . . . or lack thereof. Regret and remorse are entwined in the past. Apology faces the present and paves the way to a healthier future.

You can regret that you were caught. You can feel remorseful and wish you had acted differently. You can wish you had a rewind button, so you could replay a scenario to have a different and more positive outcome.

You cannot, however, change the past.

When you replay events over and over in your head, regret and remorse stay locked inside you.

Eventually your spiritual, emotional, and physical health may be jeopardized. You can become depressed and/or physically ill without knowing why. Regret, without positive action to reconcile the situation, can imprison you.

Avoidance is an eager companion to regret. Avoidance is the opposite of the replay button, because you do all you can to not think about the consequences and the truth of your actions. You avoid the person you offended. You avoid thinking about It as much as possible. Soon your conscience may become numb and you make similar errors in judgment. You establish behavior patterns that leave a wake of hurt behind you.

The political arena is often the stage where some elected officials have danced carefully around any admission of wrongdoing, until forced to admit the truth. Former President Bill Clinton notoriously denied details of alleged extramarital affairs, to both his family and the public, until more and more evidence emerged supporting the truth of the allegations. What should have been a private admission of regret and apology to his family, instead became sensational media coverage throughout the world. His denials caused further humiliation to his family and the women with whom he had relationships. His actions also caused embarrassment to himself and others; profound distrust in his character; and very costly legal maneuvering through subsequent charges of cover-up, lying, and possible grounds for impeachment. All this . . . because he did not have the courage and awareness to privately, and then publicly, say "I'm sorry" until forced to do so.

If you listen, you will hear how often people think they are apologizing when, in fact ,what they are really saying is that they *regret* being caught.

Angela Wilder, ex-wife of NBA player James Worthy, recalled her reaction when they confronted his infidelity. She stated, "I really have a fuzzy memory about ever hearing 'I'm sorry'. What sticks in my mind is him saying, 'I've put myself in a very bad situation.'" While his words of regret might have been true, they were not a sincere apology to his wife.[1]

Pete Rose had a brilliant baseball career until 1989, when he was barred from the game for life for gambling on baseball teams while a manager for the Cincinnati Reds. For years he denied the charges, despite mounds of evidence that were produced. In 2004, he wrote a book in which he admitted he had lied, and indeed, *had* bet on baseball teams, including the Cincinnati Reds. His lack of sincere apology and contrition for his illegal activities, and for his many years of denial and accusations toward those he had falsely accused of lying about him, only deepened the resolve of many to question his eligibility for the Baseball Hall of Fame.

As a player, his accomplishments alone might have gained him entry into this prestigious honor. However, for the ballplayers who conduct themselves honorably at all levels, not just on the field, but with integrity, honesty, and character in their personal lives, Pete Rose continued to be a questionable candidate for the Baseball Hall of Fame. His words seemed to indicate that he was sorry he was caught, but not that he was sorry for his actions.

Feelings of regret, remorse or avoidance keep the focus on *you*. Courageously facing these feelings can allow truth to emerge and the focus to shift. The situation is not about you alone. With new awareness toward another, you can begin to take steps to truly make amends.

A wonderful byproduct of saying, "I'm sorry" is the example it sets for others to release and extend their own power . . . the *power to forgive*.

While your apology does not guarantee that the road ahead will be easy, the path may be clearer, because you have brought light for the journey forward.

Chapter Three

No one ever choked to death from
swallowing his pride.

~ UNKNOWN

EVEN AT a young age, we have the ability to offer
an apology to help someone and ourselves. But
for some reason, almost instinctively, many
children withhold their apologies and refuse to admit
they did anything wrong.

As a result, parents must teach and guide children
to act with compassion and to admit their mistakes,
even if they were unintentional. Do these parental
words sound familiar?

"Say, 'You're sorry.'"
"Say it like you mean it."
"What do you say?"

Often the child's response is a reluctant or belligerent "Sorry" (you know the tone) . . . because they do not want to apologize to anyone.

We often carry this same behavior into adolescence and adulthood, skirting responsibility for our actions. When interviewed by *Time* magazine as one of the 2002 People of the Year, Sherron Watkins was asked why the upper management of Enron did not admit mistakes to protect employees, investors, and the company. Using her daughter's actions as an example, she replied, "My three-year-old won't say she's sorry. She'll sit in time-out forever! It's ingrained in human nature to fight and argue." [2]

Such a defensive posture typically only makes a difficult situation worse.

There are abundant examples of stubborn behavior, refusal to accept responsibility, and to express sincere remorse, in politics, business, and personal relationships. Many people are so adept at justifying their behavior that they no longer hear their once clear inner voice that told them to 'fess up' and apologize.

The avoidance of apologizing carries significant consequences. Situations can escalate when there is no apology. Yet difficult situations can also be diffused by one's willingness to accept responsibility and demonstrate a desire to rectify the matter with an apology.

A high school instructor and one of his students had a verbal altercation over the student's perceived defiant behavior. The instructor later regretted his loss of temper and self-control. He called the young man, and his parents, and apologized for his behavior, assuring them that he realized he could have handled the situation differently. His telephone call demonstrated leadership, ownership and integrity, and the family involved appreciated it. The instructor's apology also won him the admiration of the student, who eventually became more respectful toward others and toward himself.

On a larger scale, there are many examples of international situations that could have been eased if an apology had been extended to the injured party sooner rather than later.

In 2001, the U.S. military submarine, USS *Greeneville*, performed an emergency surfacing drill, and accidentally rammed and sank the *Ehime Maru*, a Japanese fisheries teaching vessel, off the coast of Hawaii. Nine Japanese men and teenagers were killed in the accident. This tragedy was compounded when some U.S. leaders initially chose to express "regret" and offer "sympathy". The survivors, the victims' families, and the Japanese government pressed U.S. government officials to additionally say "I'm sorry."[3]

The words we use make a difference.

According to *The Japan Times*, "Equally important . . . has been the way in which (Commander Scott Waddle) has handled himself during the investigation. Like any good commander, he took full responsibility for the events that occurred that fateful day. Against his lawyer's advice, Waddle testified during the hearing *without being granted immunity* (italics mine). His efforts to speak directly to the families of the victims have gone a long way to diffusing the anger and hurt that followed the accident. He has also expressed his desire to visit them in their homes in Japan, a gesture that should also help . . . Without proper handling, this incident could have seriously damaged the (U.S.-Japan) alliance."[4]

Throughout history, some civic organizations and religious denominations have experienced periods of great shame and turbulence over scandals by leaders who did not admit, or apologize for, their actions.

In 1993, seventeen-year-old Dontee Stokes told a therapist that Rev. Maurice Blackwell had touched him in inappropriate ways for three years. Without witnesses or physical evidence, however, the charges were dropped. In 2002, as more stories emerged about sexual abuse by some Catholic priests, Stokes became more visibly troubled and drove to Blackwell's residence. After requesting and not receiving an apology from the priest, the young man shot and wounded him.

Following this incident, Blackwell's superior, William Cardinal Keeler, reportedly admitted that Blackwell was "credibly accused of abuse" in 1993; and Keeler eventually forced the retirement of Blackwell. Curiously, however, the Cardinal, through his spokesperson, reportedly had no plans in the aftermath of the shooting to apologize personally to Stokes or his family for his lack of earlier intervention.[5]

This is just one example in which abdication of responsibility and authority can have wide ripple effects throughout many lives. True leadership acts with courage when situations require moral and legal attention. True leaders also act with compassion for the victims, who deserve justice, apology, and other healing and supportive resources.

The United States has a peculiar adversarial judicial system in which accusing others—without accepting personal responsibility—is rampant. Amazingly, several states have actually passed laws that allow physicians, under their right of free speech, to say "I'm sorry" and to make statements of compassion to a patient or a patient's survivors without having the apology used against them in any future litigation.

Ironically, by acknowledging one's mistakes in judgment or action, people can often *reduce* litigation that is costly for all involved, not only monetarily and emotionally, but also in time and energy spent on such cases. The key is to understand the importance of relationships, and not be driven by fear and worry, but rather by integrity.

Excuses and defensive behavior toward patients and customers often lead to angry, expensive lawsuits, and a damaged reputation of the business or organization.

Customers or patients often do not aggressively pursue litigation if the *right* company representative contacts them in a timely way to directly, simply, and sincerely apologize for mistakes, and to assure them that corrections will be made to prevent the same occurrence from happening again. People understand that no one is perfect . . . it is the defensiveness and cover-up that make people twice wounded and angry.

So, if we know that an authentic apology can avert negative consequences and can enhance positive relationships, why on earth don't we use this power more often?

Chapter Four

> It's always possible that I'm wrong,
> but that's never at the top of
> my list of possibilities.
>
> ~ ASHLEIGH BRILLIANT

THERE ARE many reasons why people do not apologize. Worry, fear, and pride are often the main barriers to apologizing.

According to a *USA Weekend* article by Dennie Hughes, "research shows that apology is a huge point of contention between the sexes." Hughes interviewed author Deborah Tannen, who has explored the communication differences between men and women. "Men often think in terms of winning and losing . . . which means not admitting any wrongdoing, and by no means apologizing." Women, on the other hand, require an apology in order to move on. This conditioning stems from how we are raised. "Girls are taught that saying 'I'm sorry' is a courtesy; boys equate it with having to say 'uncle', where giving in is a public humiliation." [6]

It is no wonder, then, that as adults we struggle with conflict resolution, owning up to our mistakes, and taking actions that demonstrate our regret. Expand this thinking further and you realize why people and nations are constantly at war!

Often, fear of appearing vulnerable and weak drives your decision not to apologize. If you admit you made a mistake, will the other person hold it over you? Will they punish you? Will they be angrier than they were before you apologized? Will they make you feel small, while they act smug and self-righteous? Why bother opening yourself to those possibilities when you can remain silent and go on as if nothing has happened?

Ah, but these scenarios imagine the worst. Instead, you can visualize better and more advantageous outcomes:

Perhaps you will be rewarded in unexpected ways rather than punished by negative responses.

Perhaps your relationship will deepen and forgiveness will flow in abundance.

Perhaps you will receive an apology in return for actions that offended you.

Perhaps you will just feel better for having done the right thing.

Sometimes people do not apologize because they want to sift through an experience and reflect on their actions. When they finally realize they should apologize, so much time has passed they convince themselves it is too late. They think it won't make a difference. They promise themselves to do better next time and not behave in the same way.

Rest assured, there *will* be a next time . . . and their pattern of delayed response will probably continue because they have not experienced the positive energy that is exchanged when people humble themselves to say "I'm sorry" in a sincere and timely manner.

Some people are too stubborn to apologize. They will only apologize *after* the other person has said "I'm sorry." If this sounds familiar, realize that you forfeit your courage and leadership when you wait for someone else to make the first step.

For example, a person feels pushed by another to his/her limit. Both wait for the other to apologize. Days pass in silent resistance. Any meaningful interaction is avoided. Begrudging attitudes fly back and forth. The situation occurs in families, the workplace and in neighborhoods. Precious time and trust are lost between people . . . because both parties refuse to initiate greater understanding through an apology.

Another reason people might not apologize is that they *assume* the other person *knows* they are sorry; i.e., "Love means never having to say you're sorry." If you love me, I know you did not mean it. I know you regret what you did and are sorry. I know you will try not to do it again.

Do not be fooled into believing there is no need to apologize. Whether it was someone close to you or not, your actions have damaged trust. Your apologetic words and actions can mend wounds and keep them from festering.

If you assume that someone knows you are sorry, what do they assume about your lack of responsible actions? Without your apology, they might assume you do not care about the harm you caused, and the resentment builds a wall—not only between you, but also a wall within that is hard to dismantle.

Assumptions have been the death of many relationships. By being clear and brave with your apology, miracles can result.

Sometimes it is just too hard to apologize. Maybe you did the unthinkable. An error in judgment caused irreversible damage to someone. A conscious decision you made resulted in far-reaching sorrowful consequences—for you and for others. You simply cannot bring yourself to apologize because you think what you have done is too grievous to acknowledge to anyone. How could they possibly accept your apology?

Do not allow the negative voices to be louder than the voice within you that has the truer power . . . that doing what is right and good will make a better difference, eventually, for another and for you.

Those who have lost a loved one by another's hand or action, wait to hear an apology.

An abused child waits to hear an apology.

The person treated with disrespect waits to hear an apology.

They not only *need* to hear it, they *deserve* to hear it—in order to heal, to forgive, and to live.

By releasing the energy of an apology, your soul can lighten and free you to set sail in a new direction. This energy also allows the other person to feel incredible relief and the refreshing breeze of new possibilities.

Maybe you think you were in the right and there is no need to apologize. You may be correct ... that the other person was at fault and you should not apologize.

Too often pointing blame elsewhere is an easy target that frequently misses the mark. Spend time to replay the situation in your mind. Do you see anything in your behavior that you would change if you could?

Would it be your words?
Your actions?
Your reaction?
Your timing?
Your viewpoint?

There may truly be nothing for which you need to apologize. It is important, though, to take the time to examine things closely and be responsible for that which you need to own.

A woman who had a disagreement with her adult daughter stated, "I know I was right . . . but it was for *the way I was right*, that I need to apologize to my daughter."

My parents had a wise saying that helped us gain perspective when my siblings and I felt wronged or righteous: One of them would say "I'll hold your high horse while you dismount."

While we did not like admitting that we had anything to do with an argument or problem—it was someone else's fault—their words had a way of making us consider our own actions, and thus be a part of the solution.

Chapter Five

> A stiff apology is a second insult. The injured party does not want to be compensated because he has been wronged; he wants to be healed because he has been hurt.
>
> ~ G.K. CHESTERTON

WHILE APOLOGIZING can sound simple in theory, we have thus far explored how truly difficult it can be. Therefore, it is important to consider the following guidelines to apologize effectively.

- An expression of apology must be sincere and without qualifications.

- An apology should be specific and stem from your own awareness; not because you feel *forced* to acknowledge that something you said or did resulted in hurting someone.

- Apologies are not purchased. They are courageous extensions of yourself, apart from any material item you may feel tempted to buy in place of your words of contrition.

⌒If your apology is timely, all the better . . . however, *whenever* you decide to apologize, the important fact is that you have chosen to take this step.

A sincere apology indicates that you take responsibility for your actions and harm caused to another as a result. Your awareness of your actions also infers you do not want to repeat the behavior.

Abusive people often *seem* sincere in apologizing after the damage is done. They may feel regretful . . . but only for the moment. If an improvement in their behavior does not follow, they should not be believed or trusted. The abuse will continue unless *consistent* and *positive* actions are demonstrated.

Many relationships remain troubled for far too long because one desperately wants to believe that the abuser's apology indicates that he or she will stop the abuse. The opposite too often occurs. Without personal accountability and responsibility, the cycle of harm sadly continues.

Apologizing without qualifications is essential. When you say, "I'm sorry, *but* . . ." you qualify your apology with misfocused excuse or blame. *But* is a divisive word. It separates the words you are saying into two different camps . . . what you feel you should say, i.e., "I'm sorry," and the reality of what you really want to say, i.e., "I am not really responsible. It is not my fault."

When a supervisor says, "You did a good job, but . . ." the employee does not believe the "good job" part of the statement, because he only hears the typically negative words that follow *but*. Any initial positive feedback is thus effectively erased.

An apology expressed in this way causes the same reaction. The phrase "I'm sorry, but . . ." can be heard as defensive, self-justifying, and lacking in personal accountability. A person does not really hear the apology; he or she only hears the latter negative part of the sentence. An already difficult situation becomes worse, often to the bewilderment of the person who apologized.

By using a linking word, such as *and*, instead of *but*, you can build a bridge to better communication. The phrase "I am sorry and . . ." allows the other person to be more open to hearing your sincere intent.

It is also helpful to say simply, "I am so sorry." Period. No clauses, excuses or justifications offered. Your sincere words, without any qualification or insinuated blame on someone or something else, will be most effective.

Some people apologize in ways that diminish any sincerity. Their apology is generic, not specific. "I'm sorry, *all right?*" or "I'm sorry for *whatever.*" These words ring hollow and abdicate responsibility. They essentially say "I know you are angry, but (there is that *but* word again!) since I don't know (or want to admit) what I did wrong, let's just move on." Such a feeble attempt to apologize lays more brick and mortar to the wall of anger and resentment.

Why bother apologizing if you are not specific as to what action you regret?

The criminal may be behind bars (i.e., forced to be accountable) and the victim will still feel that justice was not served because the prisoner has not acknowledged any wrongdoing. Regardless of the type of offense, a sincere apology freely offered by the criminal, and not coerced by the court, can be a healing balm to a victim's wounded body, mind, and spirit. It can also, ironically, be liberating to the prisoner.

Frequently people will apologize with the words "I'm sorry you feel that way" (can you hear again the *but* that almost always follows?). We must not apologize for how another person feels. People are entitled to the feelings they have. You can, however, apologize for what you *did* that contributed to the reason they may feel the way they do. "I'm sorry I ignored you." "I'm sorry I could not apologize sooner." "I'm sorry for my actions." Specifically owning your behavior, and not the other person's response to it, is a vital step toward any reconciliation and self-discovery.

Some people apologize frequently for situations over which they have no control. Instead of *specific* situations, *most* situations become a reason for the person to say, "I'm sorry." These frequent apologetic responses dilute the power of an apology.

If you catch yourself apologizing for situations for which you are not truly responsible, nor accountable, think for a moment. Is it a habit that you have unconsciously adopted? Once you are aware, you can develop alternative, more appropriate, and honest responses.

When something is not your fault, nor under your responsibility, you can choose your words with care. You might wish for something that did not happen. Then say so. "I wish you had gotten the job" instead of "I'm sorry you didn't get the job." Your actions did not cause the other to not get the position, so there is no need to apologize.

If a parent disciplines a child for wrongful behavior, is mom or dad sorry they demonstrated a consequence for the child's behavior? Probably not. Do they wish that things had not come to this outcome? Probably so. The reality is that the parents are holding the child accountable for behavior and choices, thus teaching a child that there are consequences. Since any consequence should be tied to the behavior, and not harmful to the child, it is not necessary to apologize that you caught your son or daughter making unhealthy choices. You are parenting wisely.

Do you think you can purchase an apology and assume someone will know you are sorry by your gift? Send a dozen roses? Buy an expensive dinner or piece of jewelry? A dream trip, or tickets to a pro game? Think again.

Extravagant gestures cannot truly take the place of an apology. They can be an *extension* of your apology, but not a replacement. Your words and attitude are still the most powerful statement and symbol of your conviction. What you say on the card, or when you offer the other person the tickets, is the greater gift. Without your personal expression of apology, your plan can backfire. The item alone will seem like a bribe, or will be a painful reminder, rather than a heartfelt peace offering to express your regret and hope for healing.

A wayward husband may buy his knowing wife a diamond necklace as a means of buying back her affection and trust. Without his heartfelt apology in words and action, she will probably hate the necklace and never wear it.

A person may receive a large monetary settlement for an accident, yet still yearn to hear words of apology from the person who caused the accident. The financial award alone does not demonstrate personal accountability, which may be of greater importance to the victim than money.

Having sex can be another way of trying to "buy" forgiveness without truly apologizing. Making love after an argument can be wonderful and healing *only* if the partner has first expressed remorse in another meaningful way. Sex in itself is not a substitute for sincerely apologizing. If you use sex as an escape, rather than as loving closure and hope for the future, your partner can feel manipulated. Submersed ill will and distrust in your relationship may then continue.

There are several aspects to consider in the timeliness of an apology. Your apology may closely follow the incident you regret. Sometimes, for a variety of reasons, it simply cannot.

In whatever timeframe it is offered, your apology needs to be extended with consideration of where and when you apologize to someone.

Give thought to the impact of your words on the other person and help them hear you in an atmosphere that is ideally conducive to confidentiality and true listening.

Sometimes you may feel the need to apologize, and without realizing it, catch the other person off guard. Letting the person know that you have something important to tell them . . . asking for time to talk to them . . . helps them respect your thoughtfulness in considering their feelings, and affects the way in which they can receive your apology.

The *right* time and the *right* words do not happen randomly. You make them happen by focusing energy and thought on what will be most helpful for the other person.

Trust your instincts. If you truly consider what you need to say or do, and consider the other person, the timing will probably be just right for your message to be received.

One final guideline to apologizing: Avoid what a friend fondly calls a "proactive" apology. When her brothers were young, they would say, "I'm sorry, I'm sorry, I'm sorry," and then proceed to punch one another the same number of times.

While we might smile at this childish scenario, as adults we sometimes also use the same method. We apologize first, before we initiate the harm to someone, and think that our "advance" apology will smooth the troubled waters that result. They will not, and they should not, because harmful intent is the opposite of a sincere apology.

Chapter Six

> A man should never be ashamed to own
> he has been in the wrong, which is but
> saying . . . that he is wiser today than
> he was yesterday.
>
> ~ ALEXANDER POPE

WHATEVER THE reason you have not apologized, it has been your decision, your choice, not to do so. And of all the choices that you have in this lifetime, you can decide to use the power of an apology now, as a significant, life-changing force, with results that lie beyond your immediate vision.

The key to unlocking this power is to remember that apologizing requires an *outward* expression of regret, remorse, or sorrow for your actions. Your apology can take shape in a variety of forms.

Words of apology, carefully chosen and shared directly in writing or verbally, take the most courage. Who hasn't struggled with finding the right words or timing, only to be frozen with fear or hesitation that no words are good enough; no timing will afford the best opportunity to extend an apology?

If you do not worry about finding the *right* words, and instead focus on just two words—"I'm sorry"— perhaps you will find it easier. Believe that. Once you sincerely say "I'm sorry," other healing words will follow.

If you do not worry about finding the *right* time, and instead, you *create* the time to privately tell someone you are sorry, perhaps time will not lapse into the next month or the next year without extending your apology.

Prepare to be amazed at the results of using your courage in this way.

One couple discovered new awareness of the power of apology in their marriage. They described the powder keg of emotions that had built each time an apology was not forthcoming.

A typical occurrence might be as ordinary as her husband blaming the family for his lost keys, only to later find them in his gym bag. Since he did not apologize to them for causing frantic searching for his keys, the episode became tinder, added to the pile of past similar experiences.

His wife also admitted a similar pattern of not apologizing to him when her behavior or words were hurtful. The resulting anger and resentment on both their parts were damaging to them individually and to their marital relationship.

As they each realized this destructive pattern, and renewed their commitment to one another with greater understanding, they discovered hope in saying the words "I'm sorry."

A written form of apology can be uniquely effective. By writing, you can give more thought to what you want to say. The person receiving a note or letter of apology also receives the gift of being able to read your words again, thus allowing the depth and breadth of your intention to take hold.

A man was legally advised not to apologize to a family whose child was hurt as a result of an accident, for which the man was partially responsible. Following his conscious, however, he wrote a letter to the family stating he was sorry for his part in what had happened. To the amazement of all involved, that note of apology freed all of them from their heavy emotional chains of sorrow and regret. While the sadness about the accident would never be erased, it seemed to be eased, and they each experienced new hope for their futures.

A word of caution: If you have written your expression of apology, do not assume that the other person received it. Lost letters are not uncommon. It is very important that you assure that anything that you wrote arrived at its intended destination.

Meaningful touch, when words are at a loss, can express your apology.

One mother and her preteen son argued about home rules and in exasperation both gave up on further communication for the night. Shortly after he had gone to bed, she regretted losing her temper, and tiptoed into his bedroom. In the darkness, she simply, gently held his hand. He, in turn, gently squeezed her hand and the two of them quietly reconciled for several minutes, without a word being spoken. Their sincere gesture of holding one another's hand, said more than words at the time could express. Through touch, they both conveyed their regret and apology for angry behavior and words. As a result, they each had a good night's sleep and experienced a new start in the morning.

In 2003, during the early days of the U.S. war in Iraq, United States soldiers exemplified apology in action. With tensions high, U.S. soldiers were faced with a car speeding toward them. Despite warnings to stop, the car kept advancing and the soldiers shot at the car, not realizing until too late that the car carried members of a civilian Iraqi family who were fleeing the war torn area. News footage of the soldiers' anguished faces, and their subsequent interaction with the grieving Iraqi survivors, was poignant to watch. With verbal language a barrier, the soldiers demonstrated compassion and regret to the Iraqis through body language, eye contact, and helpful, respectful actions to assist those who were hurt. The Iraqi survivors, even in their grief, seemed to understand through the soldiers' nonverbal communication that it was a terrible accident.

In the irony of every war, there are many examples of apology, honesty, courage, and kindness in the midst of unimaginable conditions. And therein lies hope.

Winston Churchill, known for his stubbornness, and his wisdom, was reportedly once seen at a dinner party, subtly "walking" his knuckles on the table toward his wife. When questioned by a dinner guest, Clementine Churchill stated that her husband's gesture was his way of apologizing to her for an earlier transgression, his knuckles representing his bent knee of apology.[7]

Actions, beyond words, can result in forgiveness.

As mentioned earlier, do not assume that too much time has passed and that it is too late to say you are sorry. The only time it is really too late to apologize is after your death. Your apology now, while you have the opportunity to express it, is important.

While those who wait to receive your apology may initially feel angry and say it is too late, they *will* be grateful to finally hear your words.

They may wonder what took you so long; why you could not tell them sooner; and they may not, at first, feel gratitude toward you. However, they will still feel relief toward the universe, at having finally heard your expression of apology.

In whatever way you express that you are sorry—with your voice, with a letter, with your touch, with your action—believe that your sincere apology will change an important corner of the world and will touch lives in ways that you never could imagine.

Chapter Seven

How wonderful it is that nobody need
wait a single moment before starting
to improve the world.

~ ANNE FRANK

I LISTEN for the stories. They are many and the
situations are different, yet often the common
thread is the lack of apology and how lives are
adversely affected.

I have also been profoundly moved by stories in
which someone finally, sincerely, says "I'm sorry."
These words offered another human being the
closure, the healing, and the confidence that life
could be restored in some way, on some level.

These stories are miraculous because every time life
is transformed for the better, it is a miracle. Each life
then impacts other lives in a new way. People can
experience a reawakening of their spirit—and that is
life-giving.

A young man speeding in a car killed a beloved wife and child of another man. The husband/father of the victims sought punishment and the harshest legal consequence possible for the man who was responsible. Finally, several years later, upon personally meeting the young man in prison, the widower heard the words he had desperately needed to hear: words of apology. He realized he did not need or want to hear reasons why the accident occurred—but he very much needed to hear the man say he was sorry. A floodgate of tears and remorse resulted for both of them. Together the surviving husband/father and the young man decided to make the tragedy radiate goodness. They began speaking together to high school students about the consequences of poor judgement choices when driving. Their heart-wrenching testimonies have touched lives in positive ways that they will never truly know or see. They are making an important difference in their own lives, and in others' lives, because an apology was finally shared and heard.[8]

Pumla Gobodo Madikizela, a South African psychologist and author, served on Archbishop Desmond Tutu's Truth and Reconciliation

Commission after the overthrow of apartheid. She interviewed Eugene De Rock, a white South African commander of the state-sanctioned apartheid death squads who was sentenced to 212 years in jail for crimes against humanity. During the interview, he stated that he wanted to meet with the widows of some of the men who were murdered under his command, to apologize privately to them. Imagine facing the man responsible for the murder of your loved one. Yet one widow later stated, to her own amazement, "I was profoundly touched by him."[9]

That is what the power of apology can accomplish. There are many, similar stories that are astonishing, brave, and inspirational lessons for all of us.

While you risk taking this important step of apologizing, understand that when you say, "I'm sorry" to someone, what the other person chooses to do with your apology is outside of your control.

The perfect, or expected, outcome may or may not result.

There may be anger.

There may be outward rejection of your words or actions.

Regardless of what happens, *believe* that you have acted wisely and that your apologetic words or action are all that are within your control.

While you may not see an immediate healing or reconciliation, your apology is still honorable and loving and right. Your courage and respect for others, through your sincere apology, will work toward the greater good—eventually.

Remember, also, the importance of apologizing to yourself . . . for losing self-control, for disappointing or offending or hurting yourself or others in any way. Your personal apology to yourself is vital in order to give yourself new hope and healing—and to help you be able to apologize to others.

We can learn that our life choices have universal consequences.

We can change, and free others to change, if we accept responsibility for our actions.

It is our awareness, and our subsequent choices, that will facilitate that change.

As a survivor of any crime, insult, and harm, you are entitled to words of apology, in order to heal.

Yet, if you never receive the gift of an apology, which you need and want so desperately to hear, you can still use another power that you possess. You can use the power of forgiveness . . . at whatever level of forgiveness you can offer . . . because it will be an action for your own well-being.

Usually the anger and rage you feel toward someone else, hurts only you and the people who care about you.

Extending forgiveness to someone, without receiving an apology first, is an attitude of heart that says, "I deserve to move forward, and accept healing from other sources for this pain/hurt/anger."

Angela Shelton, author, screenwriter, actress, and documentary filmmaker, searched for healing from the early sexual abuse she and her siblings suffered at the hands of her father. As an adult, she courageously wrote him about her memories, yet received no response. Years later, while filming her documentary, *Searching for Angela Shelton*, she confronted her father about her painful memories. Her father feigned ignorance of the abuse ("I made stupid mistakes. I wouldn't do that.") and he refused to apologize and to ask for her forgiveness. She said sadly to the camera, "All I wanted is some closure."

Instead, Angela found healing through the women and friends she met along the way in her documentary. She stated to an incredulous reporter that she forgave her father. "Forgiveness," she said, "has nothing to do with him. It has everything to do with me. I'm not an abuse victim. I'm an abuse survivor."[10]

By empowering herself, this accomplished woman learned that her life can finally be healthier and stronger.

Do not allow someone else's lack of courage to apologize to determine how you will proceed with your life. You are *entitled* to live your life with whatever strength and happiness you can discover within you; and to experience support from those who care about you, through whatever has happened.

What you decide to do with your life is your challenge and also your choice.

There are resources.

There are people who want to help you.

Seek them.

Accept them.

Teach them.

Learn from them.

And be open and watchful for the ways an apology might come to you in unexpected ways from unexpected sources.

Whatever you believe spiritually, there is an awareness that resides within you that knows you and desires that you be well and whole.

Live in that awareness.

In the lovely movie, *Simon Birch*, there is a tender, crucial scene. Simon, a young child of unusual abilities and disabilities, has accidentally killed someone very special in his life. He is heartbroken, and stands alone in the middle of a bridge. With anguish that sounds like it comes from his toes, he hoarsely yells to the universe, "I'M SORRY."

Our world needs a Simon Birch apology for all the hurts, the violence, the misunderstandings, the wrong choices, the pain, the greed, and the exploitations that exist.

Decide *now* to use your power to extend an apology and to bring healing to others and to your life—not only for today, but for generations to come.

Your life, and the lives of others, are that important.

It is your choice.

Choose wisely.

Guide to a New Beginning

I N ORDER to begin the process of apologizing, consider these steps:

    ⚘ Who comes to mind when you think about apology? _____

_____

_____

    ⚘ What situation comes to mind when you think about apology? _____

_____

_____

    ⚘ What has prevented you from apologizing or hearing an apology? _____

_____

_____

🖙 List three steps you can take to begin the healing journey of apology for another and for yourself. _____

_____

_____

_____

_____

🖙 Write down the timeline in which you will take positive action . . . beginning today. _____

_____

_____

_____

_____

🖙 Identify a source of support, strength, and encouragement for you each step of the way.

_____

_____

_____

_____

_____

Deliberately facing the fears of "what if" can empower you to move through them, toward healing action.

☞ Ask yourself "What is the worst that can happen if I apologize?" And then ask yourself "What helpful action can I take if the worst did happen?" _____

_____

_____

_____

_____

☞ If you yearn to hear an apology, ask yourself "What is the worst that can happen if I never hear the words 'I'm sorry'?" and then, "What could happen instead, to restore my heart and mind?" _____

_____

_____

_____

_____

Know that I am with you in spirit on your journey toward wholeness.

Every story is important. If you wish to share your experience on the subject of apology, I welcome you to e-mail me at:

balconypub@freeway.net

Endnotes

1. ABC 20/20, 8/8/03. "For Many NBA Stars, Marriage is No Slam Dunk."

2. *TIME* magazine, 12/30/02-1/6/03, "Persons of the Year interview", page 59.

3. CNN.com *In Depth Special* 3/1/01.

4. *The Japan Times* online 4/18/01.

5. *TIME* magazine, "Making a Priest Pay" by David Van Biema, 5/27/02.

6. *USA Weekend*, "Speak No Evil" by Dennie Hughes, 5/4-6/01.

7. *Guidepost Daily Devotional*, November 29, 2003, reflection by Fay Angus.

8. *NBC Dateline*, "When Worlds Collide"; 9/3/03. and *PEOPLE* magazine; "Forgiven Sins" by Thomas Fields-Meyer, Kristin Harmel and Jeff Truesdell; 11/18/02.

9. *TIME* magazine, "The Quality of Mercy" by Lance Morrow, 1/27/03.

10. *CBS 48 Hours Investigates;* Bill Lagatutta "Searching for Angela Shelton"; 3/10/04.

About the Author

SHEILA QUINN SIMPSON earned a bachelor and Master of Arts degree at Michigan State University. Her career includes working as a speech pathologist, hospice administrator, and her current role on staff at Davenport University. She is also a speaker on issues related to well-being.

Sheila was presented with the 2004 Athena Award for community leadership and service.

She lives in Northern Michigan with her husband, Charlie, where they raised their three children.

Order Information

To order a copy of *Apology: The Importance and Power of Saying, "I'm sorry"* please send a check or money order made payable to:

Balcony Publications
P.O. Box 2032
Gaylord, Michigan 49734

Individuals and organizations wanting to order ten or more copies, telephone 1-877-780-2588 for volume discount information.

Prices
$12.95 each plus $3.50 for shipping and handling (for the first book, plus $1.75 for each additional book sent to the same address).

If you would like to contact the author, you may write to her at the above address or via e-mail at:
balconypub@freeway.net